A New True Book

OLYMPICS

By Dennis B. Fradin

TABLE OF CONTENTS

 CHILDRENS PRESS, CHICAGO

Archaeologists have unearthed many of the buildings and temples at Olympia in western Greece.

THE ANCIENT GREEK OLYMPICS

In 776 B.C., some men went to Olympia, in western Greece, to run in a race. It was to be a run of 200 meters (about 660 feet).

The crowd cheered as a young man named Coroebus crossed the finish line. On that summer day nearly 2,800 years ago, Coroebus became the first recorded Olympic champion.

Thousands of years ago, the Greeks had a great civilization. They created beautiful art works. Many Greeks considered the body to be as important as the mind.

By 1000 B.C. the Greeks enjoyed many sports. They had foot races and chariot races. They boxed and

Statues recall two ancient sports:
the armed boxer (above) and the
discus thrower (left)

wrestled. The Greeks
believed that the gods and
spirits of the dead enjoyed
watching sports. Sporting
events were held at
funerals and at religious
festivals.

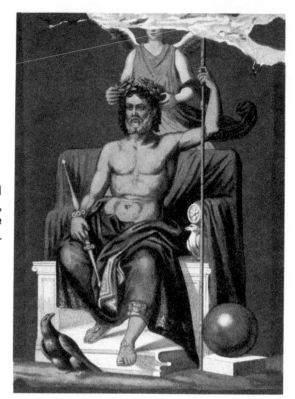

Zeus, king of all the Greek gods, was honored at the ancient Olympics.

Zeus was the king of the Greek gods. About three thousand years ago a shrine to Zeus was built in the Valley of Olympia. Sports were part of the religious ceremonies held there. The first recorded sporting event at Olympia was that race won by Coroebus in 776 B.C.

The Greeks decided to hold the race at Olympia every four years. More events were added. In 724 B.C., the first 400-meter race was run. Four years later the first 4,800-meter race was held. Wrestling, boxing, and chariot races were added. So were

This illustration shows how ancient Olympia looked. Forty thousand people came here to watch the athletes compete.

special events for boys aged twelve to seventeen. Because the sporting events were held in the Valley of Olympia, they became known as the Olympic Games.

In those years, Greek cities often fought each

other. However, a truce
was declared before the
games. It was illegal to
attack an athlete, coach, or
fan on his way to the
Olympic Games.

On the day when the
five-day Olympics began,
the stadium was packed.
All forty thousand in the
crowd were men. Women
weren't allowed to watch
or compete in the Olympics.

After ceremonies to honor Zeus, the sports began. Each event had only one winner. There were no second or third prizes. For a long time, the winner's prize was a crown made of olive branches and leaves.

When an Olympic champion returned home, parades were held in his honor. Statues of him were built. Songs and poems were written about him.

Wrestling

The ancient Olympics
had many great
champions. Milo of Croton
was one of the greatest.
First he won the boys'
wrestling title. Then from
532 to 516 B.C. he was
adult wrestling champ five

13

Boxing

times. Milo was said to be
so strong that he once
picked up a bull and
carried it around the
Olympic stadium.

Another great champion,
Theogenes of Thasos, won

titles in two sports. He won the title in boxing—a violent sport in which many men died. Theogenes also won the pankration title. The pankration was a brutal sport that combined wrestling, judolike moves, and boxing. (Theogenes was so proud of his victories that he named his son Disolympios, meaning Twice-Olympian.)

During the second century B.C., the Romans conquered Greece. As Greece lost its power, the Olympic Games fell apart. The religious part of the games was forgotten. So was the idea of fair play. The Greek Olympic Games ended in A.D. 394. They had been held for nearly twelve hundred years.

Opening cermony at the 1980 summer games in Moscow, U.S.S.R.

THE MODERN OLYMPICS

The stadium and other Olympic buildings stood empty for centuries. From time to time raiders stole statues and other items from them. In the sixth century the buildings were smashed by an earthquake. Then floods dumped twenty-five feet of sand on them. The Olympic buildings lay buried beneath that sand for more than fourteen hundred years.

In 1766 Richard Chandler, an Englishman, found the ancient site. German scientists uncovered the ruins in 1881.

Close-up of the ruins at Olympia, Greece

Those ruins reminded people of the ancient Olympics. They also gave Baron Pierre de Coubertin, a Frenchman, the idea to start a new series of Olympic Games.

De Coubertin believed
that sports were healthy.
He also hoped that if
nations got together for
sports, they might be less
likely to make war on
each other.

The International Olympic
Committee was formed.
They organized the games
and made rules. A main
rule was that the athletes
had to be amateurs. This
means they could never
have earned money from sports.

The first modern Olympic Games were held in Athens, Greece in 1896—more than 1,500 years had passed since the last Olympic event.

The plan was to hold the Olympics in a different city of the world every four years. Athens, Greece, was picked to host the first modern Olympics.

21

Thirteen nations sent 285 athletes to Athens in 1896. Some events were the same as the ancient ones. Others were new. James B. Connolly, an American, won the first event—the hop, step, and jump, or triple jump. Connolly became the first Olympic champion in 1,502 years.

Women couldn't enter the 1896 Olympics. That was changed for the next Olympics, in Paris in 1900.

Another change came in 1924. The games were then divided into two parts—Winter and Summer. The Winter Olympics are held the January or February before the Summer Games.

Opening ceremony (left) at the 1980 winter games in Lake Placid, New York. Skier (below) competes in jump.

The International Olympic Committee picks the cities for each set of games. They pick the sports for the games, too.

HOST CITIES OF THE MODERN OLYMPIC GAMES

Year	Summer Olympics	Winter Olympics
1896	Athens, Greece	
1900	Paris, France	
1904	St. Louis, Missouri, U.S.A.	
1908	London, England	
1912	Stockholm, Sweden	
1916	Not held because of World War I	
1920	Antwerp, Belgium	
1924	Paris, France	Chamonix, France
1928	Amsterdam, The Netherlands	St. Moritz, Switzerland
1932	Los Angeles, California, U.S.A.	Lake Placid, New York, U.S.A.
1936	Berlin, Germany	Garmisch-Partenkirchen, Germany
1940 and 1944	Not held because of World War II	Not held because of World War II
1948	London, England	St. Moritz, Switzerland
1952	Helsinki, Finland	Oslo, Norway
1956	Melbourne, Australia	Cortina, Italy
1960	Rome, Italy	Squaw Valley, California, U.S.A.
1964	Tokyo, Japan	Innsbruck, Austria
1968	Mexico City, Mexico	Grenoble, France
1972	Munich, West Germany	Sapporo, Japan
1976	Montreal, Canada	Innsbruck, Austria
1980	Moscow, Russia	Lake Placid, New York, U.S.A.
1984	Los Angeles, California, U.S.A.	Sarajevo, Yugoslavia
1988	Seoul, Korea	Calgary, Alberta, Canada

Here are the sports scheduled for the 1984 and 1988 Olympics

SPORT	OLYMPIC WINTER	OLYMPIC SUMMER
Archery		X
Athletics (track & field events: 16 for women, 24 for men)		X
#Baseball (men only)		X
Basketball		X
Biathlon (men only—shooting and cross-country skiing)	X	
Bobsled (men only)	X	
Boxing (men only)		X
Canoe & kayak (women kayak only)		X
Cycling		X
Diving		X
Equestrian		X
Fencing		X
Field hockey (men)		X
Field hockey (women)		X
Figure skating	X	
Gymnastics		X
Ice hockey (men only)	X	
Judo (men)		X
Judo (women)		
Luge	X	
Modern pentathlon (men only: fencing, horseback riding, pistol shooting, running, swimming)		X
Roller skating (might be on 1987 program)		
Rowing		X
Shooting		X
Skiing, Alpine & Nordic	X	
Soccer football (men only)		X
Softball		
Speed skating	X	
Swimming		X
*Synchronized swimming (women only)		X
**Table tennis		X (1988)
Team handball		X
#**Tennis		X (1988)
Volleyball		X
Water polo		X
Weightlifting (men only)		X
Wrestling (men only)		X
Yachting		X

Sport includes both men and women, unless otherwise stated.
  * New on the program for 1984
 ** New on the program for 1988
 # Demonstration sport for 1984

CEREMONIES AND AWARDS

The modern Olympics, like the ancient ones, have a number of ceremonies. The opening ceremonies are very impressive.

No matter where the games are held, the athletes from Greece enter the stadium before those of other countries. This reminds people that the Olympics began in Greece.

Audience displays the Olympic flag.

An official of the host
country declares the games
"open." The Olympic flag
is raised. It shows five
interlocked rings. Each is
a different color—black,
blue, green, red, and yellow.
The rings represent Africa,
Asia, Australia, Europe, and
North and South America.

Next comes the lighting of the Olympic flame. Weeks before the games, relays of runners carry a burning torch from Olympia, Greece, to the site of the Olympics. If oceans must be crossed, the flame is sent by boat, plane, or laser beam. The final runner brings the torch into the stadium and lights the Olympic flame,

Lighting
the flame
begins the
Olympic Games.

which burns throughout the
Olympics. (The flame is
another reminder that the
games began in Greece's
Valley of Olympia.)

Doves are released as the opening ceremonies end. These birds have long been a symbol of peace.

As they soar above the crowd, they remind people that the Olympics are held to promote world peace.

The games last for several weeks. Most events have elimination rounds before the finals. For each final event, three medals are given. The first-place medal is gold; second place is silver; third place is bronze.

Bruce Jenner (above) accepts his gold
medal for winning the Decathlon.
Close-up of the front and back of
the 1896 gold medal (right).

As the winners receive
their medals, the flags of
their countries are raised.
A band plays the national
anthem of the gold medal
winner's country.

GREAT MODERN OLYMPIC CHAMPIONS

The modern Olympic Games have produced many great champions from all over the world.

Three athletes have won nine gold medals each in their Olympic careers. Paavo Nurmi, a runner from Finland, won his nine gold medals from 1920 to 1928. Larisa Latynina, a Russian gymnast, earned

Jim Thorpe (left),
Paavo Nurmi (middle),
Mark Spitz (right)

hers between 1956 and
1964. The American
swimmer Mark Spitz won
his nine gold medals in
1968 and 1972.

Jim Thorpe, an American Indian, was one of the greatest of all Olympic athletes. In 1912 he won gold medals in the pentathlon and the decathlon. Thorpe later played professional baseball and football.

Muhammad Ali, Joe Frazier, George Foreman, and Leon Spinks all won gold medals in boxing. All

Leon Spinks (left) Muhammad Ali (right)

four later became world
champion pro boxers.

In the 1924 and 1928
Olympics, the American
Johnny Weissmuller earned
a total of five gold medals
in swimming. He later

Sonja Henie (left) Eric Heiden (right)

played Tarzan in the
movies. Sonja Henie of
Norway won three gold
medals for figure skating
between 1928 and 1936.
She, too, became a movie
star. In 1980 Eric Heiden,
an American, won five gold
medals for speed skating.

Wilma Rudolph (left) Nadia Comaneci (right)

Nadia Comaneci of Romania was one of the youngest Olympic champions. In 1976, at age fourteen, she won three gold medals in gymnastics.

The Americans Ray Ewry and Wilma Rudolph had to overcome handicaps to win their medals. Both were crippled as children. Both had to work hard just to learn to walk. Both made themselves into amazing athletes. Between 1900 and 1908 Ray Erwy won eight gold medals in jumping events. Wilma Rudolph, a great runner, won three gold medals at the 1960 Olympics. For that she was nicknamed "the World's Fastest Woman."

The Jesse Owens story is one of the most famous in Olympic history. In 1936 Owens went to Berlin, Germany, to represent the United States. Adolf Hitler, Germany's leader, said that blacks, Jews, and other minorities weren't as good as the Nazi Germans. Jesse Owens, a black man, proved him wrong.

Jesse Owens

Owens won gold medals in the 100-meter dash and three other track and field events. His victories are proof that skill is the only thing that counts in sports.

MAKING THE TEAM

More than one hundred countries and eight thousand athletes compete in the Olympics. How does one get to be an Olympic athlete?

First, you must be an amateur. This rule governs athletes of all nations.

Next, you must make the team. Each nation has an Olympic committee. The committee holds selection

Athletes who make the team have their travel, food, and housing expenses paid by the Olympic Committee.

trials or tryouts. The best athletes at the selection trials make the team.

To get invited to the selection trials, an athlete must have done well in college or amateur sports.

When athletes are asked how they made the Olympic team, they often say: "I practiced a lot." For example, a swimmer may spend hours each day in the pool. A runner may cover many miles each day in practice runs.

Why do athletes want to compete at an event that offers medals instead of money? "To bring honor to my country," some say. "To prove I'm the best in the world," many have said.

The Olympic Creed adopted by Baron Pierre de Coubertin states: "The most important thing in the Olympic Games is not to win, but to take part, just as the most important thing in life is not the triumph but the struggle. The essential thing is not to have conquered but to have fought well."

Do you love sports? If so, perhaps one day you'll compete in one of the world's greatest sporting events—the Olympic Games.

WORDS YOU SHOULD KNOW

A.D. – this refers to the years on the Christian calendar after the birth of Christ

archery (AR • cher • ee) – the sport of shooting with a bow and arrow

athlete (ATH leet) – a person who competes at sports

award (ah • WARD) – a prize given to one who does well

B.C. – this refers to the years on the Christian calendar before Christ was born

biathlon (by • ATH • lon) – a Winter Olympics event combining shooting and cross-country skiing

ceremony (SAIR • ih • moh • nee) – an act held to honor someone or something

champion (CHAMP • eeyun) – the first-place winner

chariot race (CHAIR • ee • ot) – a race between horse-drawn carts held in the ancient Olympics

committee (kuh • MIT • ee) – a group of people

competition (cahmp • ih • TISH • un) – the process of playing against others

decathlon (dih • CATH • lon) – an Olympic contest consisting of ten separate track and field events

elimination rounds (e • lim • in • AYE • shun) –competition held to reduce the number of people involved in the finals

equestrian sports (ih • KWESS • tree • an) – horseback riding

Greece (GREESS) – a European country where an advanced civilization developed thousands of years ago

international – involving a number of nations

kayak (KYE • ack) – a light, narrow boat

luge (LUJ) – a sledding event held in the modern Winter Olympics

meter (MEE • ter) – a length of 39.37 inches, or a little more than 3 feet

modern Olympics – the games that have been held since 1896

modern pentathlon (pen • TATH • uh • lon) – a contest consisting of five events: cross-country running, swimming, pistol shooting, fencing, and horseback riding

Olympia (o • LIM • pyah) – a valley in western Greece

pankration (pan • KRAY • shun) – an ancient, brutal sport that combined wrestling, judo, and boxing

selection trials (seh • LEK • shun • TRYLEZ) – tryouts held to see who will make a country's Olympic team

stadium (STAY • dee • yum) – a place where athletic events are held

truce (TROOSS) – the stopping of war for a certain time

yachting (YAWT • ing) – the racing of small sailing ships

Zeus (ZOOSS) – king of the ancient Greek gods